Dunstaffnage Cas
& Chapel

Doreen Grove
Principal Inspector of Ancient Monuments

Bird's-eye view of Dunstaffnage Castle from the west. Dunstaffnage Chapel is hidden in the woods bottom left.
(Courtesy of John Anderson, Highland Image.)

A Guided tour of Dunstaffnage Castle & Chapel

Dunstaffnage Castle repays the visitor with an eye for detail. The mighty fortress may look solid and all of a piece, but down the centuries it has undergone significant change.

This tour begins with a walk around the outside of the castle walls, for these contain important clues as to how the place was used. The tour of the interior begins on page 9.

The guided tour ends with a visit to the castle chapel (see page 14). Visitors may find a visit to the exhibition on the upper floor of the visitor centre rewarding before setting out on their tour.

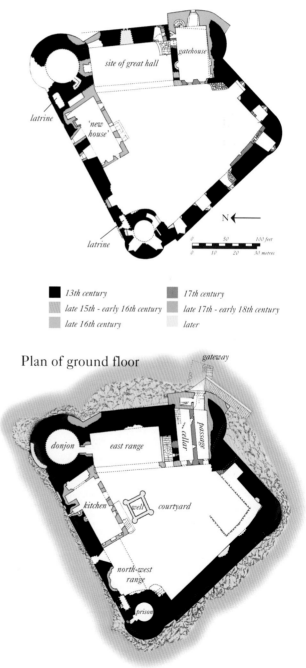

Plan of first floor

site of great hall

gatehouse

latrine

'new house'

latrine

N

■ *13th century*	■ *17th century*
late 15th - early 16th century	*late 17th - early 18th century*
late 16th century	*later*

Plan of ground floor

gateway

donjon *east range* *passage* *cellar*

kitchen *well* *courtyard*

north-west range

prison

Contents

THE CASTLE FROM THE OUTSIDE

The entrance front of the castle.

Dunstaffnage Castle stands on a promontory jutting out from the southern shore of Loch Etive at the point where it meets the Firth of Lorn. It thus guarded the seaward approach up the loch to the Pass of Brander, and thence into the heart of Scotland. Dunstaffnage Bay, sheltered from the prevailing westerly winds by the promontory, also made a good anchorage. Indeed, yachts still make full use of the place where Duncan of Lorn's galleys once moored.

The forbidding **castle walls** rise sheer from the summit of a rock outcrop that is fully 9 m above ground level. These walls, built of local rubble and with courses of larger blocks laid on edge, continue upwards for another 6 m and more. At the base of the walls, outlets drained water from the courtyard within, whilst openings irregularly spaced just below the wall tops similarly drained the wall-walks and the roofs of the buildings behind. The original tops of the walls are now gone, so there is no evidence to show whether they were battlemented or covered with a timber superstructure.

As you approach from the visitor centre, the severity of the wall ahead betrays the builder's concern that this landward side was the most vulnerable to attack. It has no openings in it, other than **narrow arrow-slits**. These were subsequently blocked up and small **gunholes** - some round, others 'keyhole-shaped' - inserted, probably around 1600.

The original castle, built around 1220, had no projecting corner towers, just a massive wall, almost 3.5 m (11 ft) thick, skirting the edge of the rock. The corner nearest the visitor centre was never given a tower and shows how the whole castle would have looked when first built. Not that you would have seen any stonework; on the wall to the left of the entrance stair are traces of harling, a white lime render that originally coated all the walls, making the castle even more conspicuous on its rocky perch.

THE ENTRANCE

The entrance we see today dates from the later fifteenth century, when the Campbells became owners of the castle. It replaced an earlier entrance in the same position, for which scarcely any evidence remains other than the natural fissure in the rock at this point (see page 9). The new entrance also removed almost all trace of the earlier corner tower, the curved wall of which is visible to the left of the bow-fronted projection housing the present entrance.

The round-headed entrance **doorway** is set within a pointed arched recess. How one reached that doorway in years gone by is unclear, for the present **stone stair** dates only from the eighteenth century when a 'new house' was built inside. There must have been a bridge, for the north end of the present stair uses one side of a drawbridge pit, whilst the fragmentary remains of the other side can be detected in the wall beneath the doorway, and in the ground running away to the east. The steps, or a ramp, leading up to the outer end of that drawbridge have yet to be discovered through excavation.

The crow-stepped and harled building rising up above the entrance battlements is part of the **gatehouse** rebuilt in the late sixteenth century; the window above the entrance doorway dates from the same time.

THE GREAT HALL AND DONJON

The stretch of wall to the right of the entrance has one of the finest architectural features of the castle. High up in the wall is a **double-lancet window**, decorated with dogtooth ornament; an identical window graces the chapel. To its right is a similar but plainer window. Both hint that they lit something grand behind, and there was - the great hall, the main public room in the castle. Both windows were subsequently blocked, and a small gun-loop inserted in the former.

On the far right of the wall stands the largest of three **corner towers** added to the castle walls around 1250. At the bottom, the stonework is battered outwards to form a sloping base, perhaps to make the tower more difficult to undermine; it has the appearance of being an afterthought. The size of the tower, and its position adjacent to the great hall, suggest that it served as the donjon, housing the lord's private apartment. However, it has been so altered and repaired down the centuries that little remains of its original arrangement; several openings visible in the interior are no longer visible here on the outside.

The entrance into the castle (left) and the donjon (right) that originally housed the lord's private accommodation. The great hall, the main public room in the castle, was between them.

THE NORTH-WEST RANGE AND WEST TOWER

The stretch of wall along the back (north-west) side of the castle illustrates the long domestic use this quarter of the castle has seen. The present fringe of trees masks the views out from the castle, making it difficult for us to appreciate how important this area was to the residents. The windows in the donjon and adjacent north-west range would have provided spectacular panoramas across the Firth of Lorn, to the distant peaks of Morvern and Mull.

Immediately adjacent to the donjon is a large **latrine chute**, corbelled out from the wall-face; this served the rooms in the donjon. A similar, smaller **chute** to its right served chambers in the range. Most of the other openings are square, and later. However, high up on the right side is another fine **double-lancet window** that must have lit a room of some quality behind. The vertical line in the masonry to the right of this window suggests that the original corner of the castle wall stopped at this point; the fissure in the rock below supports this. The west tower is clearly an addition.

The **west tower** had three floors of accommodation which you will see better from the inside. Here on the outside can be seen several tall, **narrow arrow-slits**, some with fishtail bases (to widen the archer's field of fire); they have mostly been blocked or shortened. Also prominent is another projecting **latrine chute** that served the upper floors of the tower. The **drain** or chute at the base of the wall served the pit-prison in the base of the tower. Perhaps this was not a spot to linger in the 'good old days'!

Now return to the entrance.

The gatehouse from the castle courtyard, and (inset) the entrance passage. The original size of the entrance passage is expressed by the pointed arch in the gatehouse harling. The passage was subsequently reduced in width.

THE CASTLE FROM THE INSIDE

THE ENTRANCE PASSAGE

Immediately inside the entrance door, to the right, is a deep, **narrow slot** in the masonry; this held the long timber draw-bar that helped secure the two-leafed door. Next to it is a **guard room**, or porter's lodge; a hint of the boredom of his task is visible on the outer door jamb, where **scratch marks** bear witness to the many idle hours he spent sharpening his weapons.

The **entrance passage** is much narrower than when first built in the late fifteenth century, for the wall on the right, beyond the guard room, was only inserted in the seventeenth century. The original passage was at least twice as wide, and those passing through entered the courtyard through a wide, pointed-arched doorway, the outline of which can be seen from the courtyard. The restricted passage provided an extra **storage cellar** here at ground level, but perhaps more importantly better security; note the **gunhole** and **defensive slits**, for use by defenders stationed in the cellar.

Now go into the courtyard and look back at the white lime-harled gatehouse.

THE GATEHOUSE

The gatehouse is in the keeping of the captain of Dunstaffnage (see page 27) and is not normally open to visitors. It dates from the sixteenth century, and was probably built by the then captain to replace the antiquated lordly accommodation within the donjon.

It comprises three floors, with a single room to each floor. Access to these upper floors was originally by an external stair, and the stub of masonry to the right (south) of the gatehouse may be the remains of it. The present access is from an external stair to the left (north) of the gatehouse; this was probably constructed in the early eighteenth century as part of the wholesale remodelling of the castle accommodation.

The **first floor** was most probably a reception room and outer dining room. It has a good-sized fireplace in the north wall, and is well lit from west and east. A narrow **stair** in its north-east corner leads down into the **cellar** off the entrance passage, suggesting that this may have been the wine-cellar. Another wider **spiral stair** in roughly the same position leads to the **upper two floors**, which together functioned as a private suite for the captain. The first has two fireplaces, indicating that this single space was formerly divided into two rooms. That at the rear (east), entered directly from the stair, was probably a withdrawing chamber, where the captain's family could relax in greater privacy and eat their everyday meals; that facing onto the courtyard would have been the captain's bedchamber. The top floor, or garret, is entirely featureless apart from the dormer windows, which are late additions (see page 14).

The entrance doorway from below.

10   *Alexander MacDougall, lord of Lorn, presides over a trial in his great hall at Dunstaffnage, around the year 1290;*
a reconstruction illustration by David Simon. The tower looming up in the background is the donjon, housing his private rooms.

THE GREAT HALL

The east range, to the left of the gatehouse, once housed the most important room in the castle, the great hall. This was the hub, around which almost all castle life revolved. When built around 1220, as an integral part of the original castle, it may have been linked directly with the accommodation in the north-west range, where the lordly accommodation was most probably located. But when the three corner towers were added around 1250, the direct link between the two ranges was broken by the largest of those towers, the donjon, which probably now housed the lord's private suite.

The arrangement of the great hall is now difficult to interpret. It was certainly on the upper floor, above a ground-floor storage cellar(s). Perhaps the most important clues are the two double lancets windows (later blocked) that brought light into the hall from the east. The finer of the two, adjacent to the gatehouse, is better viewed from the outside (see page 6); it has dogtooth decoration identical to windows in the chapel. The other, not visible at all on the inside, was plainer. Their respective positions pose an anomaly, for we would normally expect the more elaborate window to be at the top end of the great hall, where it would enhance the dais, or raised platform where the lord sat. This may indicate that some lordly accommodation existed in the early gatehouse before the donjon was built.

It is a great pity that the west wall of the great hall, facing onto the courtyard, is now gone, for it would have contained more nice windows, perhaps a good-sized fireplace, a grand entrance door and external forestair. The great hall, however, largely lost its purpose by the seventeenth century, and the fact that a fireplace was built into the ground-floor doorway linking it with the donjon suggests that it was included in the drastic remodelling undertaken in the early eighteenth century.

Go through the doorway into the donjon.

THE DONJON

The donjon was the largest of the three towers added to the original castle around 1250. It was built for two reasons - to provide archers stationed within a better view of the outer faces of wall, and to furnish the lord with more, and better, accommodation.

The donjon was originally probably three storeys high. The **ground floor**, only recently archaeologically excavated and opened to visitors, served as a **storage cellar**, and had no direct link with the upper floors, though there may have been a trapdoor linking the two. The excavations proved that the donjon was definitely added to the castle and not an original feature, for the original wall was found cutting across the centre of the floor. They also showed that the ground floor had three arrow-slits, similar to those still visible in the west tower. The upper two floors (not now accessible) together formed the lord's private suite of rooms, a hall and chamber. In the spiral stair in the west wall was an **open-chuted latrine,** better seen from outside.

One of the latrine closets projecting from the back wall that once served the lord's apartments.

The roofless 'new house' in the north-west range, created in 1725 from an earlier kitchen, and (inset) the fine fireplace on its first floor. Flora MacDonald may have been held prisoner here in 1746. In the foreground is the elaborate nineteenth-century wellhead marking the location of the all-important castle well.

THE NORTH-WEST RANGE

The original accommodation in the north-west range was altered out of all recognition in 1725, when the captain remodelled it as a free-standing, two-storeyed house. That it formerly housed high-status accommodation, however, is clear from the fine double-lancet window at first-floor level adjacent to the west tower. This is no longer visible here on the inside because it was subsequently blocked and hidden behind a sixteenth-century chimney flue, but it can still be admired from outside the castle.

What happened to those lordly rooms after the donjon was added around 1250 is unknown. Certainly by the sixteenth century, part of the ground floor seems to have been rebuilt as a **kitchen**; the **large fireplace** in the wall next to the donjon, and some (at least) of the square openings through the castle wall, date from this time. Then came the conversion of the range into the '**new house**'. The upper floor of the kitchen became two rooms, accessed from the courtyard by a stone **forestair.** A late-nineteenth-century photograph shows this 'new house' in a poor state of repair. But what it also shows are the three dormer windows that formerly graced this courtyard elevation. (They were subsequently taken down in 1903 and rebuilt at the top of the gatehouse.) The date and inscriptions on them, and on one surviving window lintel, confirm that the 'new house' was built for Aeneas Campbell, the eleventh captain, and his lady, Lillias Campbell, in 1725.

The elaborate stone **wellhead** in front of the 'new house' dates from the nineteenth century, although the well itself was no doubt in use from the outset in the early twelfth century.

THE WEST TOWER

The west tower, like the donjon, was once three storeys high but not so large on plan as the donjon, suggesting that it was not as important. It may have served as guest accommodation or as apartments for the lord's senior henchmen. The modern timber access leads into the **first floor**. This may have been a **guard room**, for a draw-bar once secured the door and there was a **pit-prison** below (still filled with debris and not yet excavated). Two narrow, fishtailed **arrow-slits** penetrate the walls. The upper floor seems always to have been accessed directly from the wall-walk rather than from within the tower.

From the west tower, continue up to the wall-walk and enjoy the fine views.

A cut-open reconstruction illustration of the west tower showing how it might have originally been used (David Simon).

THE CASTLE WALLS

A continuous **wall-walk** around the top of the landward-facing castle walls enabled the garrison to keep watch on this more vulnerable side of the castle. Much of the wall-walk has been repaired to make it safe for visitors, but small areas of original stone slabbing have been kept. At the end of the wall-walk you will get a close sight of the **1725 dormer windows**, removed from the 'new house' in 1903.

The three dormer windows on the top of the gatehouse. They originally graced the 'new house' in the north-west range, built in 1725 by Aeneas Campbell, the eleventh captain.

Now return to the courtyard.

The stretch of castle wall below the wall-walk, to the right of the gatehouse, has a variety of recesses which originally gave access to tall, **narrow arrow-slits**. They were all subsequently altered, mostly around 1600 to fit them for guns. Although there are no buildings along this west side of the courtyard, it does not necessarily follow that none ever existed; only with excavation will we find out.

Don't forget to visit the chapel, in the woods close by the castle, before you leave.

Dunstaffnage Chapel as it might have looked around 1250 (David Simon). The timber screen (now gone) divided the space into chancel and nave, and had a rood, or crucifix (not shown), above the linking doorway. Inset; one of the fine paired-lancet windows in the chancel.

DUNSTAFFNAGE CHAPEL

Dunstaffnage Chapel is an extraordinary building that perfectly illustrates the wealth and sophistication of its builder, Duncan MacDougall. No other chapel of this date in mainland Scotland can match it for quality.

The inspiration for the architecture derives from Irish churches, but several features can be found at other churches in the area, including the nunnery on Iona, and Ardchattan Priory, beside Loch Etive, also founded by Duncan (see pages 30-31).

The chapel is a single space, 20 m long, formerly divided by a timber screen into nave and chancel. Sadly, the decoration around the three **entrances** is fragmentary, but it is likely that all had elaborate arched doorways. The major provision of light is into the **chancel**, where the altar would have been bathed in sunlight streaming through the three **paired-lancet windows**. Those worshipping in the **nave** would not have read during services, even supposing they could; hence just a **single lancet** in each of the north and south walls, positioned to light the rood, or crucifix, on the timber screen; a socket for fixing the screen is visible in the south wall. Externally, all the windows are chamfered, and the eastern one on the south side has bold dog-toothed ornament similar to that on a window lighting the castle's great hall. Internally, the chancel windows are very fine, with widely-splayed arches, and sides enriched either with nook shafts or dog-toothed ornament. The nave windows are much simpler.

Little is known of the chapel, other than that it was a family chapel, serving the lord's household in the castle, and never a parish church as such. In 1740, after the chapel had become ruinous, the Campbells of Dunstaffnage built a burial aisle against its east gable, with a nice neo-classical entrance. It is crowded with fine memorials to members of the family.

Dunstaffnage Castle and Bay from the south west.

THE STORY OF
DUNSTAFFNAGE CASTLE
& CHAPEL

Dunstaffnage, the MacDougall stronghold guarding the seaward approach from the Firth of Lorn to the Pass of Brander and central Scotland, is one of the oldest castles in Scotland, and a tangible link to the remarkable struggle between Scotland and Norway in the thirteenth century for the disputed territories of the Hebrides.

The acquisition of the region by the Scots in 1266 did not see the end of the disputes in the west; far from it. Until the last Jacobite Rising in 1745-6, the history of Dunstaffnage is inextricably intertwined with the incessant struggles by the Scottish monarchy and their loyal henchmen, the Campbells, to control their unruly western subjects.

FROM DUN MONAIDH TO DUNSTAFFNAGE

The name Dunstaffnage is derived from the Gaelic *dun*, meaning fort, and two Norse words *stafr*, staff, and *nes*, promontory - hence 'fort on the staff promontory'. The word staff may allude to an office-bearer of some sort.

Myth and legend surround Dunstaffnage. Some have associated it with Dun Monaidh, a seventh-century stronghold of the Scots of Dál Riata, but as yet there is no archaeological evidence to support so early a date. Should it prove correct though, it would lend weight to the legend, recorded by John Monipennie in 1612, that the Stone of Destiny, Scotland's ancient coronation stone, was brought to Dunstaffnage from Ireland and remained there until Kenneth I had it taken to Scone, in Perthshire, in 853, following the union of the kingdoms of Scotland and Pictland in the 840s. Dunstaffnage, it has to be said, seems an unlikely location for the Stone; Iona, where the first recorded Scottish king-making ceremony took place, or Dunadd, also intimately linked with the Dál Riatan kings, would seem the more likely homes.

The shift of power from west to east in the reign of Kenneth I, whether or not accompanied by the Stone of Destiny, was very real. Into the vacuum stepped the Vikings, who had first raided Iona in 795. Formal acceptance of their sovereignty over the western seaboard came in 1098, when King Edgar of Scotland ceded the region to King Magnus 'Barelegs' of Norway. In truth, neither king effectively controlled the area, for a local élite challenged the authority of both. By the mid-twelfth century, one man, of mixed Gaelic/Scandinavian descent, ruled supreme - Somerled, self-styled 'King of the Isles'. It was his eldest son, Dubhgall (or Dougall), who founded the MacDougall clan, and his grandson, Duncan, who built mighty Dunstaffnage Castle.

The 'king', a medieval ivory chess-piece, found at Dunstaffnage Castle in the nineteenth century.

Dunstaffnage Castle (right) and Chapel (left) as they might have looked when the MacDougall lords held sway over Lorn in the thirteenth century (David Simon). Their lordship was essentially a maritime one; hence the galley-house for the lord's own galley beside Dunstaffnage Bay, the chief anchorage, and the fleet of galleys sailing in from the Firth of Lorn.

A MacDougall Stronghold

Following Somerled's death at Renfrew in 1164 fighting the Scots, the Islesmen invited Dougall, his eldest son, to become 'King of the Isles'. However, they also invested Dougall's two nephews, Domnall (Donald) and Ruaidhri (Rory), with lands and power too. So began the division of the territory into three major lordships - Lorn, at the centre, held by Dougall; Kintyre and the south by Donald; Garmoran and the north by Ruaidhri. These three dynasties, the MacDougalls, MacDonalds and MacRuaris, feuded between themselves as well as with the Scottish and Norwegian kings, skilfully using their relations with the kings of England to promulgate disputes and retain power. Between them they have left an astonishing legacy of castles.

Little is known of Dougall, or where within his lordship he had his administrative centre. The architecture of Dunstaffnage Castle strongly suggests that it was begun by his son Duncan around 1220. Not much more is known of Duncan, in truth. He first appears on record around 1175 when, as a young child, he visited Durham with his father and brother. In 1224, he witnessed the foundation charter of Paisley Abbey, established by Walter, the High Steward of Scotland, an irony given that Walter's grandfather had been responsible for Somerled's death in 1164. Around 1230, Duncan founded his own monastery, Ardchattan Priory, just 6 miles (10 km) east of Dunstaffnage.

Duncan was also a man of action. In 1230, he figured significantly in the Norwegian expedition against Alexander II of Scotland that culminated in him successfully capturing Rothesay Castle from Walter Stewart; they were soon forced to withdraw, however. By 1237, he had clearly made his peace with Alexander for in that year he was the only western signatory to a document sent by Alexander to the pope. Duncan's establishment of Ardchattan Priory may have been a demonstration to Alexander of his good will.

The west tower, one of three round towers added to the original castle wall around 1250, during the 'show-down' between the kings of Scotland and Norway. The tall, narrow arrow-slits confirm the warlike intentions of the builder, Ewen of Lorn.

THE APPROACH OF KING ALEXANDER'S ARMY

Then came from west beyond the sea Ewin,
Duncan's son, and Dugald, Ruaidhri's son; and
they both endeavoured after this, that the king
[Hakon IV] should give them the title of king.

(from *Eirspennil's Hakon Hakon's son's Saga*, c.1248)

Alexander II of Scotland had turned his attention to reclaiming the lost lands in the west in the 1220s; hence King Hakon's expedition of 1230. In the 1240s, Alexander renewed his attempt, this time trying bribery; Hakon replied that he had 'no such urgent need of silver'. Then Duncan MacDougall's son, Ewen, provided Alexander with the perfect excuse to attack.

In 1248, Ewen and his cousin Dugald sailed to Bergen, in Norway, to seek the title 'King of the Isles' from Hakon; Ewen won. Shortly afterwards, King Harald of Man was drowned off Shetland, likewise following a visit to Bergen. Hakon, concerned about a breakdown in Norse control of the Hebrides, appointed Ewen to step into the breach. Ewen now controlled almost the same extensive territory as his great-grandfather, Somerled.

Alexander of Scotland would not tolerate such power on his western frontier. He gathered a great army and marched westward. During the ensuing negotiations, Alexander offered Ewen 'a much larger dominion in Scotland; and along with it our friendship', so long as Ewen ceded his four great castles, not named but almost certainly including Dunstaffnage. Ewen refused, saying he could serve two masters 'provided the masters were not enemies'. Such impertinence was too much for Alexander, who entered Argyll in strength. Alas, whilst his fleet was anchored in Oban Bay, he contracted a fever and died on the island of Kerrera on 8 July 1249.

The ensuing stalemate was broken in 1260 when Alexander III began his personal reign. Continuing where his father left off, he soon forced Hakon to intervene personally. By late September 1263, Hakon and his huge fleet were in the Clyde. But autumn gales and an indeterminate battle at Largs, on the Ayrshire coast, combined to make him withdraw. Hakon never saw his kingdom again, dying in the Bishop's Palace at Kirkwall, in Orkney. Negotiations between his successor, King Magnus, and Alexander III continued for another two years before agreement was finally reached. The Treaty of Perth 1266 brought the lands of the west back under Scottish rule once more, after more than 250 years.

Ewen of Lorn's role in these goings-on is far from clear, but given his past record, and also the fact that his 'kingship' of the Isles, with all its power and status, had been transferred to the MacDonalds, it seems highly probable that he awaited the outcome of the race before choosing which horse to back. In the end he chose Scotland, a decision reinforced by the marriages of his children into major Scottish dynastic houses. Ewen undoubtedly relished status and power, and it was most likely he who improved the castle at Dunstaffnage and built those great corner towers.

The return of Argyll to Scotland inevitably affected the status of Ewen MacDougall. He is soon being described as 'of Argyll' and that is the title his son Alexander used. With the creation of the shire of Argyll in 1293, Alexander, its first sheriff, became the chief instrument of Scottish power in the west, leaving the junior line, the MacDonalds, to continue resisting Scottish domination and taking on the title 'Lords of the Isles'.

The enthronement of King Alexander III of Scotland on the Stone of Destiny at Scone in 1249, as depicted in Abbot Bower's Scotichronicon *(c.1445). A Gaelic bard kneels at the king's feet and recites his royal pedigree. It was during Alexander III's reign that Scotland reclaimed the lands of the west. (Courtesy of the Master and Fellows of Corpus Christi College, Cambridge, ms 171, f 205r.)*

DUNSTAFFNAGE IN THE WARS OF INDEPENDENCE

'The king that stout wes stark and bauld [bold]
Til Dunstaffynch rycht sturdely
A sege [siege] *set and besyly* [busily]
Assaylit the castell it to get [win]'
(from John Barbour's *The Bruce*, 1370)

The fortunes of the MacDougalls of Argyll during the bloody Wars of Independence with England that erupted in 1296 were linked very much with those of the rivals for the throne of Scotland - the Balliols and the Bruces. The ageing Alexander MacDougall and his son, John (nicknamed 'Bacach', crippled), sided with King John Balliol, an alliance that inevitably brought them into direct conflict with Robert Bruce once the latter seized the throne in 1306.

By the summer of 1308, Bruce had sufficient strength to move against the MacDougalls. His forces came by sea and by land, and around 15

The Pass of Brander (foreground) with the northern expanse of Loch Awe beyond. The battle fought here in August 1308, and the capture of Dunstaffnage Castle by King Robert the Bruce soon after, effectively ended the power of the MacDougall lords of Lorn.

August confronted the MacDougalls' army in battle at the Pass of Brander, on the lower slopes of Ben Cruachan. John watched helpless from his galley on Loch Awe as his men were caught in a vice-like grip by Bruce and his second-in-command, Sir James Douglas. Bruce pursued him back to Dunstaffnage and laid siege to the castle.

In desperation, John wrote to Edward II of England appealing for help. He told of Bruce having up to 15,000 men against his 800, and further revealed the precariousness of his position: 'I am not sure of my neighbours in any direction.' But no relief arrived, and Dunstaffnage soon fell to Bruce. Its loss effectively marked the end of the MacDougalls' hold on power in the west. By 1309, Alexander and his son were exiles in England. Their ancestral seat in Argyll was now the property of the king of Scots.

The initials A C and L C and the date 1725 on one of the dormer windows atop the gatehouse at Dunstaffnage Castle. Aeneas was the eleventh Campbell captain of the castle, and Lillias his lady. Right: the arms of the Campbell earls of Argyll proudly display the 'Galley of Lorn'.

Dunstaffnage remained a royal castle for the next 150 years, though little is heard of the place until 1431. In that year, James I seized the castle and hanged 300 rebels sheltering therein, Islesmen who had lately defeated a royal force at Inverlochy (near Fort William).

In 1463, Dunstaffnage figured in a family dispute between John Stewart of Lorn, keeper of the castle, and Alan MacDougall, his rival; the MacDougalls had wormed their way back into royal favour in the later fourteenth century. Whilst on his way from the castle to the chapel, where he was due to marry the mother of his son so as to legitimise the heir, John was fatally stabbed, though he managed to crawl to the altar and complete his vows before breathing his last! MacDougall seized the castle but was soon evicted by a force despatched by James III. To prevent such a thing occurring again, James granted the castle and lordship to his loyal henchman in the region, Colin Campbell, first earl of Argyll.

Colin wasn't the first Campbell to have held Dunstaffnage; his forebear, Arthur Campbell, had been appointed keeper by Robert the Bruce in 1321. But now the Campbells were here to stay, holding the estate of the Crown for a yearly payment of a plaid or shawl, a red rose, a pair of gloves and two silver pennies, to be delivered at Dunstaffnage Castle on the feast of John the Baptist (24 June).

Dunstaffnage was never a home of the Campbell earls. Instead, they entrusted it to kinsmen. In 1502, Archibald, the second earl, appointed his cousin, Alexander Campbell, as constable, or captain, of Dunstaffnage, the third to hold this post. In return, the captain was bound to keep the castle in repair and readiness, with a peacetime garrison of 'six able and decent men with armour and arms sufficient for war' as well as a watchman and porter (whose bored scratch-marks we saw on the wall of the porter's lodge).

Thereafter, the Campbells, and occasionally the Scottish kings, used Dunstaffnage as a base from which to launch offensives against rebellious Islesmen, most notably of course the MacDonalds, Lords of the Isles. Expeditions in 1493, 1540, 1554 and 1625 all involved Dunstaffnage. From time to time, other rival clans witnessed Campbell justice being meted out at Dunstaffnage, most memorably in 1585 when John Cameron of Lochiel was beheaded there on the orders of the seventh earl.

The pivotal role of the Protestant earls of Argyll in the religious and civil strife of the seventeenth century brought Dunstaffnage once more into the national spotlight. The garrison held out against the duke of Montrose's royalist army in 1644, and three years later succeeded in capturing Montrose's second-in-command, Sir Alexander MacDonald,

whom they hanged from the castle battlements and then buried just outside the chapel.

During his ill-fated rising against the Catholic James VII in 1685, Archibald, the ninth earl, succeeded in landing at Dunstaffnage with a small force. Alas, the rising failed, the earl was executed and the castle set on fire by the rejoicing royalists. Their joy was short-lived, and on King James's flight into exile in 1689, the castle was returned into Campbell hands. Thereafter, it played a bit-part in the Jacobite troubles of the early eighteenth century, the highlight being the imprisonment there in 1746 of Flora MacDonald, for her part in helping Prince Charles Edward Stewart to escape. She stayed but a few days before being taken south to the Tower of London.

Flora MacDonald (1722-90) was arrested in late 1746 for her part in helping 'Bonnie Prince Charlie' to escape, and briefly imprisoned in Dunstaffnage Castle before being sent to the Tower of London. She may have been held in the gatehouse or the 'new house' in the north-west range. (Courtesy of the National Galleries of Scotland.)

The castle from the south west.

THE TWILIGHT OF THE CASTLE

Throughout all this time, few records survive of building works at the castle. The Campbells certainly made major changes to the entrance gatehouse, probably soon after they became owners in 1470, and reconstructed the domestic accommodation in the north-west range during the sixteenth century. The other big change was carried out in 1725, when the captain had the old kitchen along the north-west side rebuilt as a two-storeyed house.

An inventory of furnishings, compiled in 1767, mentions Angus Campbell's 'new house'. It also shows how much the ancient castle had the air of decay about it. The only parts then in use were the 'old tower', presumably the fifteenth-century gatehouse, and the 'new house'. The inventory does, however, give us some insight into the furnishings in a castle, albeit at such a late date. There were tent-beds and box-beds, chairs with leather, cane and rush seats, round, square and oval tables. These all added comfort to the chambers in the castle, which included 'my lord's roum' and the 'dice room' - presumably a withdrawing room or dais chamber, and not a gambling den! Closed stools had by now replaced the draughty old latrines, and among the little luxuries of life were decanters, a coffee-pot and a chocolate-pot.

The hereditary captains continued to reside at Dunstaffnage until the place was devastated by fire in 1810. The 'new house', however, continued to be occupied by a tenant until 1888, when the captain had it turned into a teahouse for entertaining guests. In the interim, the duke of Argyll, the castle's owner, expressed a desire to restore the ancient fortress to something approaching its former glory, but nothing came of it until 1903, when the gatehouse was partially restored; Edward VII donated £25 and Andrew Carnegie £100.

When the twentieth captain inherited the keepership in 1908, he too expressed a desire to restore the castle and live in it himself. The duke disagreed, and the case went to court. Four years later, the Court of Session ruled that, although the castle was owned by the duke as lord of Lorn, the captain of Dunstaffnage was its hereditary keeper and had right of residence. Alas, the Great War intervened, during which the captain spent much of his time as a prisoner of war, and the roof on the 'new house' collapsed. Although repairs were carried out on his return, the impetus had faltered, and in 1958, when the twenty-first captain succeeded, he and the duke agreed to entrust the castle into state care.

DUNSTAFFAGE CASTLE.

Dunstaffnage Castle (right) and Chapel (left) as they looked in the late eighteenth century. The gatehouse and chapel are unroofed, and the trees that now shroud the promontory have yet to spring up.

ARDCHATTAN PRIORY

In 1231, at Ardchattan, on the northern shore of Loch Etive 6 miles (10 km) east of Dunstaffnage Castle, Duncan MacDougall founded a small priory for Valliscaulian monks. He seems to have chosen this very strict order to demonstrate his allegiance to Alexander II of Scotland, for in the previous year Alexander had established the order at Pluscarden, near Elgin, in the eastern Highlands. This somewhat obscure order, formed in 1205 at Val des Choux ('valley of the cabbages'), near Dijon in France, was drawn to remote locations in France, but only ever settled outside that country in Germany and the Scottish Highlands. Besides Pluscarden and Ardchattan, there was a third priory at Beauly, north-west of Inverness.

Frustratingly little survives of Ardchattan. The priory church consisted of a small rectangular monks' choir on the east, two side arms, or transepts, each with two chapels, and a rectangular nave on the west with a single aisle on the north. The monks lived in a square cloister to the south of the church, which never appears to have had a west range, suggesting their numbers were never large. The priory was partly rebuilt in the fifteenth century, the works including a new, larger choir, and a new refectory.

In 1506, the prior, a MacDougall, was removed under something of a cloud. It is tempting to link this act to the strengthened position of the Campbells in the area. Then came the Reformation of 1560 and with it the demise of monasticism. In 1602, Alexander Campbell, the commendator (lay administrator) of the priory lands, set about converting the cloister's south range, where the refectory had been, into a private house. (This was later remodelled and enlarged in the nineteenth century, making the site as we see it today something of an intriguing

jigsaw puzzle - with many of the pieces hidden under and within the house, which remains a private residence.) The church meantime remained in use as the parish church, until a new one was built near Ardchattan manse in 1731-2. By then, the priory church had largely been appropriated by the Campbells as a burial place.

In addition to the Campbell monuments, Ardchattan possesses some very fine medieval carved stones. The oldest is a tenth-century cross-slab (see right) that may conceivably have been brought to the site from an earlier chapel nearby. More clearly at home is a good collection of medieval graveslabs carved in the West Highland tradition. Most were erected to members of the MacDougall clan. Perhaps the finest is the cross dedicated to Sir Eugenius MacDougall, who died in 1500; Dougall, his successor, commissioned the Iona-based sculptor John O'Brochlan to carve it.

The tenth-century cross-slab on display at Ardchattan Priory.

FURTHER READING

J G Dunbar 'The Medieval Architecture of the Scottish Highlands', in L Maclean (ed) *The Middle Ages in the Highlands* (1981)

R Fawcett *Scottish Abbeys and Priories* (1994)

J Lewis 'Dunstaffnage Castle, Argyll & Bute: excavations in the north tower and east range 1987-94', *Proceedings of the Society of Antiquaries of Scotland*, 126 (1996), 559-603

R A McDonald *The Kingdom of the Isles: Scotland's Western Seaboard c1100-1336* (1997)

Royal Commission on the Ancient and Historical Monuments of Scotland *Argyll, An Inventory of the Monuments. Volume 2 - Lorn* (1975)

Royal Commission on the Ancient and Historical Monuments of Scotland *Argyll Castles in the Care of Historic Scotland* (1997)

W D Simpson *Dunstaffnage Castle and the Stone of Destiny* (1958)

C Tabraham *Scotland's Castles* (2004)

F A Walker *The Buildings of Scotland: Argyll and Bute* (2000)